Editor
Janet Cain, M.Ed.

Managing Editor
Ina Massler Levin, M.A.

Editor-in-Chief
Sharon Coan, M.S. Ed.

Illustrator
Kevin Barnes

Cover Artist
Brenda DiAntonis

Art Manager
Kevin Barnes

Art Director
CJae Froshay

Imaging
Craig Gunnell

Product Manager
Phil Garcia

Publisher
Mary D. Smith, M.S. Ed.

Kindergarten

Author

Traci Ferguson Geiser, M.A.

Teacher Created Resources, Inc.
6421 Industry Way
Westminster, CA 92683
www.teachercreated.com

ISBN: 978-0-7439-8620-5

©2004 Teacher Created Resources, Inc.
Reprinted, 2008

Made in U.S.A.

Table of Contents

Introduction

The old adage "practice makes perfect" can really hold true for your child and his or her education. The more practice and exposure your child has with concepts being taught in school, the more success he or she is likely to find. For many parents, knowing how to help their children can be frustrating because the resources might not be readily available. As a parent, it is also difficult to know where to focus your efforts so that the extra practice your child receives at home supports what he or she is learning in school.

This book has been written to help parents and teachers reinforce basic skills with children. *Practice Makes Perfect: Sequencing* introduces the alphabet and alphabetical order, the concepts of before and after, sequencing events, and sequencing ordinal numbers. The exercises in this book can be done sequentially or in any order that best meets the needs of your child.

The following standards, or objectives, will be met or reinforced by completing the practice pages included in this book. These standards are similar to the ones required by your state and school district.

- Identifying uppercase (capital) and lowercase letters
- Forming uppercase (capital) and lowercase letters
- Sequencing the letters of the alphabet
- Recognizing before and after
- Identifying the sequence of events
- Using ordinal numbers to represent a sequence

How to Make the Most of This Book

Here are some useful ideas for making the most of this book:

- Set aside a specific place in your home to work on this book. Keep it neat and tidy, with the necessary materials on hand.
- Set up a certain time of day to work on these practice pages to establish consistency, or look for times in your day or week that are less hectic and more conducive to practicing skills.
- Keep all practice sessions with your child positive and constructive. If your child becomes frustrated or tense, set the book aside and look for another time to practice. Forcing your child to perform will not help.
- Help beginning readers with instructions.
- Review and praise the work your child has done.
- Allow the child to use whatever writing instruments he or she prefers. For example, colored pencils can add variety and pleasure to drill work.
- Pay attention to the areas with which your child has the most difficulty. Provide extra guidance and exercises in those areas.
- Look for ways to reinforce sequencing skills using real-life applications. In other words, play games with your child that allow him or her to practice sequencing.

Alphabet Sequencing

Each caterpillar shows a different list of letters.
Write the missing capital letters to complete each list.

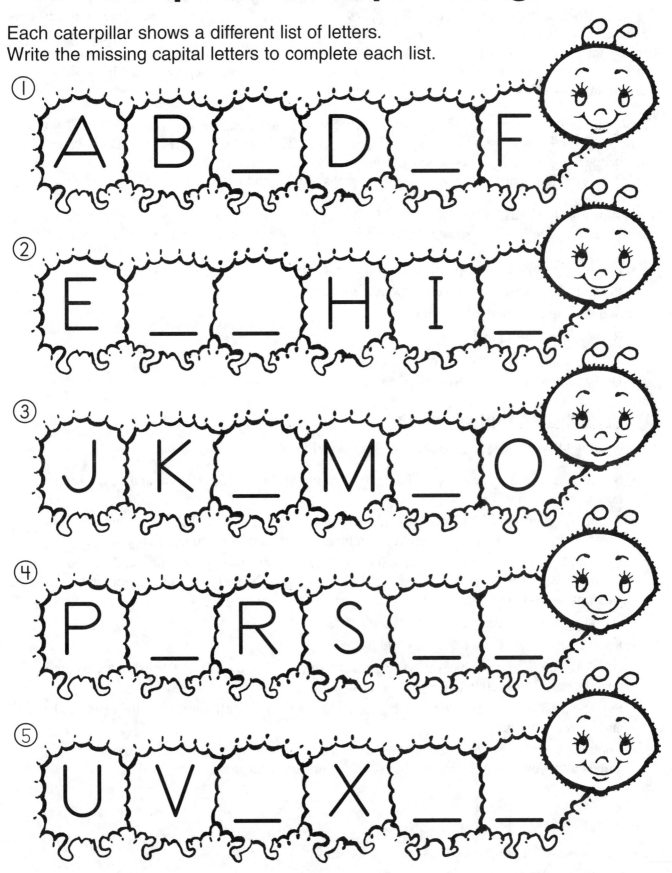

① A B _ D _ F

② E _ _ H I _

③ J K _ M _ O

④ P _ R S _ _

⑤ U V _ X _ _

Alphabet Sequencing

Each train shows a different list of letters.
Write the missing lowercase letters to complete each list.

① a b ___ d

② w ___ y ___

③ l m ___ ___

④ g ___ ___ j

⑤ r ___ ___ u

Alphabet Sequencing

Cut out the blocks on pages 6 and 7. Then put the blocks in alphabetical order.

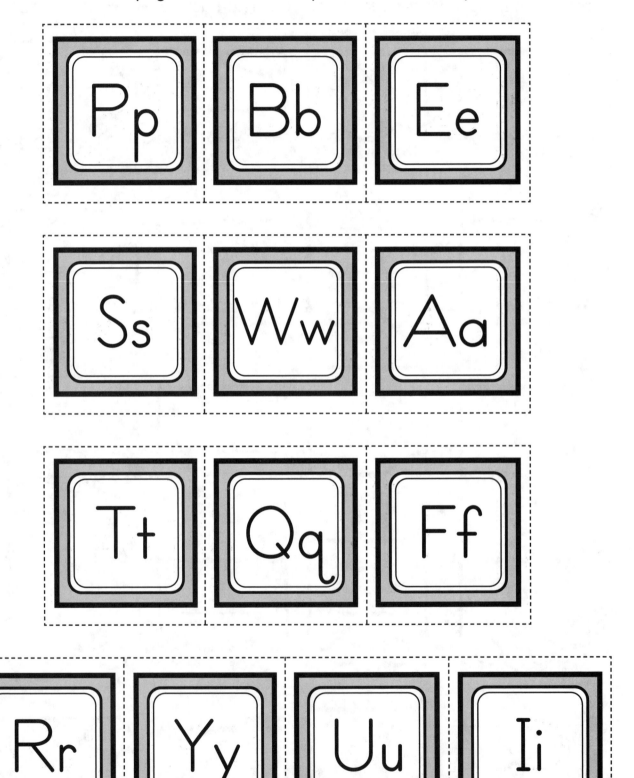

Alphabet Sequencing *(cont.)*

Cut out the blocks on pages 6 and 7. Then put the blocks in alphabetical order.

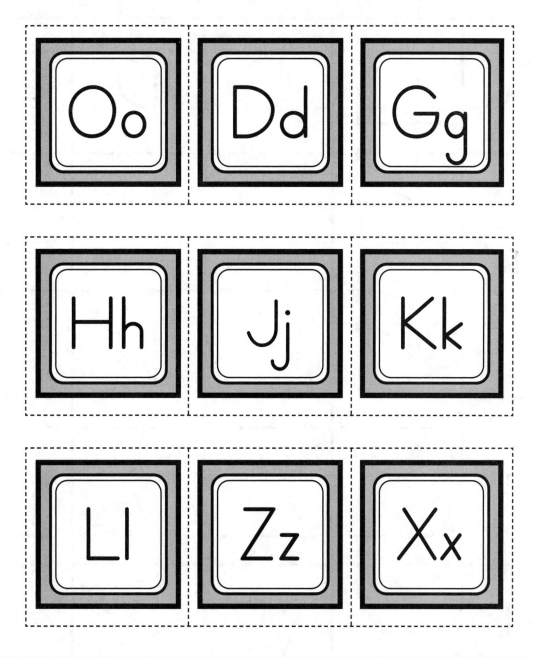

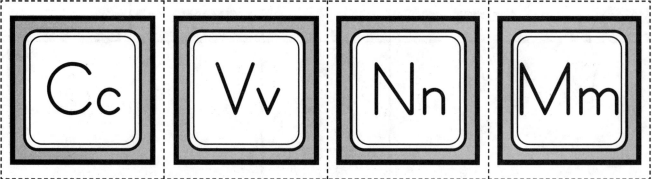

Alphabet Sequencing

Write the missing capital letters.

A	__	C	D	__
F	G	__ __	__	J
__	L	__	N	__
P	__ __	__ __	S	__
U	__	W	__	Y
		__		

Alphabet Sequencing

Each book should have a matching capital and lowercase letter on it. Write the missing capital or lowercase letter on each book. The first one is done for you.

Alphabet Sequencing

Write the missing lowercase letters to complete each list.

①   a   b   c   __   __

②   l   m   n   __   __

③   r   s   t   __   __

④   f   g   h   __   __

⑤   u   v   w   __   __

Alphabet Sequencing (cont.)

Write the missing lowercase letters to complete each list.

① _____ _____ h i j

② _____ _____ x y z

③ _____ _____ c d e

④ _____ _____ n o p

⑤ _____ _____ s t u

Alphabet Sequencing

Look at the word under each picture on pages 12 and 13. Cut out the squares with dotted lines from below. Put the squares in alphabetical order by the first letter of each word. Then glue the squares with dotted lines in the correct place.

Alphabet Sequencing *(cont.)*

Look at the word under each picture on pages 12 and 13. Cut out the squares with dotted lines from below. Put the squares in alphabetical order by the first letter of each word. Then glue the squares with dotted lines in the correct place.

umbrella

walrus

yo-yo

ball

dog

frog

heart

(Jack-in-the-box)

lion

nest

pumpkin

ring

turtle

violin

xylophone

zebra

Before and After

Look at each pair of pictures. Circle the picture that comes first.

Before and After

Look at each pair of pictures. In each box, write a **1** under the picture that comes **before** you clean up. Then write a **2** under the picture that comes **after** you clean up.

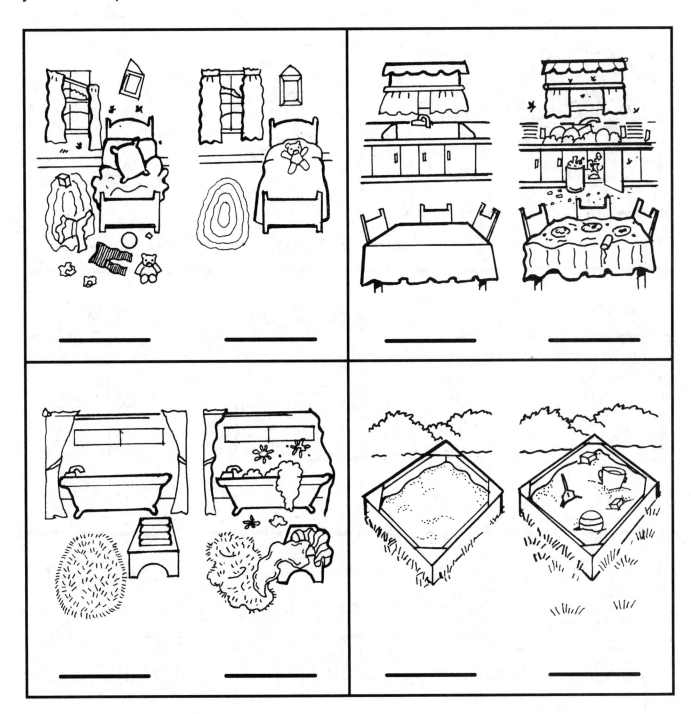

Before and After

Look at the three pictures in each row. Circle the word **Before** under the picture
that comes *before* the first picture in the row. Circle the word **After** under the
picture that comes *after* the first picture in the row.

Before   After   Before   After

Before   After   Before   After

Before   After   Before   After

Before and After

Write the numbers that come
before and **after** the given number.

Write the letters that come
before and **after** the given letter.

——— , 5 , ———　　　　|　　　——— , H , ———

——— , 7 , ———　　　　|　　　——— , B , ———

——— , 2 , ———　　　　|　　　——— , X , ———

——— , 10 , ———　　　　|　　　——— , T , ———

——— , 15 , ———　　　　|　　　——— , O , ———

——— , 19 , ———　　　　|　　　——— , L , ———

Before and After

Look at the pictures at the bottom of the page. Cut out the squares along the dotted lines. Now look at the pictures in each row. One of the pictures you cut out will go **before** the middle picture. One of the pictures will go **after** the middle picture. Glue the pictures on top of the words **Before** and **After**.

Before and After

Look at the three pictures in each row. Circle the **happy face** or **sad face** to tell how you would feel **before** and **after** the event shown in the middle of each row.

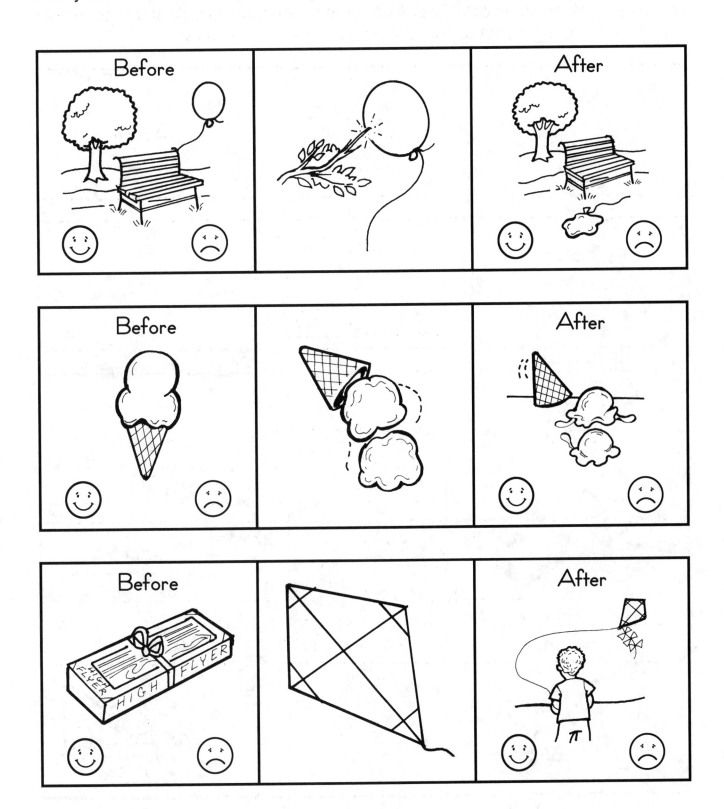

Before and After

The pictures on the left side of the page show what happened **before** the pictures on the right side of the page. Draw a line to connect the **Before** picture on the left side of the page with its **After** picture on the right side of the page.

Before and After

The pictures on the right side of the page show what happened **after** the pictures on the left side of the page. Draw a line to connect the **Before** picture on the left side of the page with its **After** picture on the right side of the page.

Before

After

Before

After

Before

After

Before

After

Before and After

Look at each pair of pictures. Circle the word **Before** or **After** under each picture.

Before   After   Before   After

Before   After   Before   After

Before and After (cont.)

Look at each pair of pictures. Circle the word **Before** or **After** under each picture.

Before   After   Before   After

Before   After   Before   After

Beginning, Middle, and End

Cut out the cards on pages 24 and 25. Find the cards with the same letter on them. Put each set of cards in order on the mat (page 26).

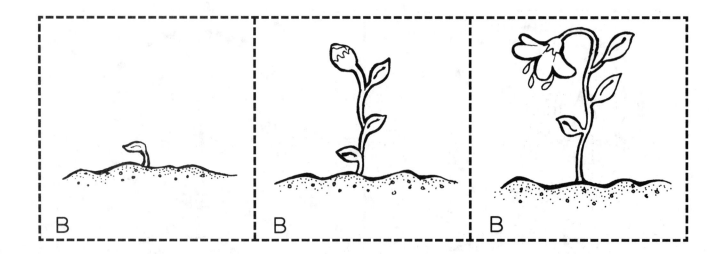

Beginning, Middle, and End *(cont.)*

Cut out the cards on pages 24 and 25. Find the cards with the same letter on them. Put each set of cards in order on the mat (page 26).

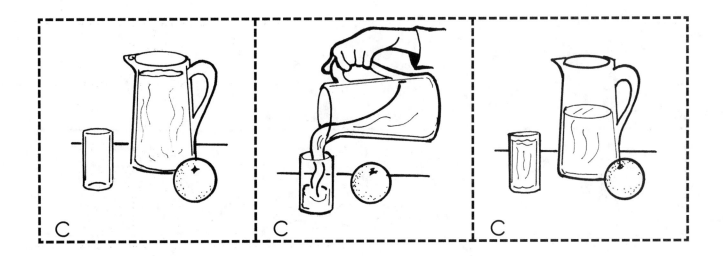

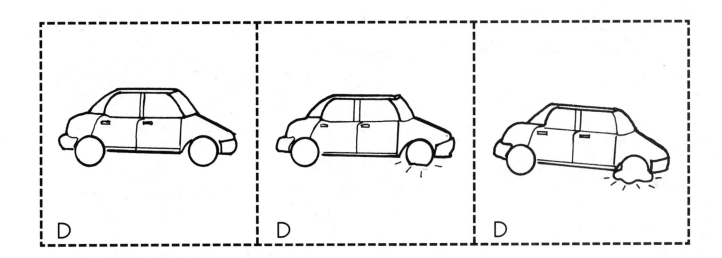

Beginning, Middle, and End *(cont.)*

Use the following mat to show the order of the cards from pages 24 and 25.

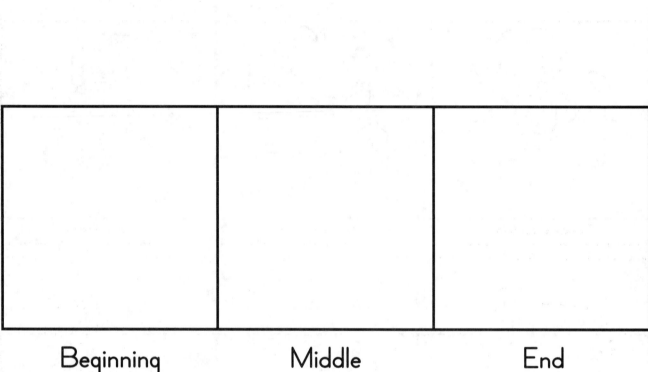

| Beginning | Middle | End |

Beginning, Middle, and End

Look at the pictures in each row.

Write a **1** under the picture that shows the **beginning**.

Write a **2** under the picture that shows the **middle**.

Write a **3** under the picture that shows the **end**.

Beginning, Middle, and End

Cut out the pictures along the dotted lines. Each set of pictures has the same symbol at the top. Put each set of pictures in order. Then read the nursery rhyme that goes with the pictures.

Little Miss Muffet, sat on her tuffet, eating her curds and whey.

Along came a spider that sat down beside her,

And frightened Miss Muffet away!

Jack and Jill went up the hill to fetch a pail of water.

Jack fell down and broke his crown,

And Jill came tumbling after.

Beginning, Middle, and End (cont.)

Cut out the pictures along the dotted lines. Each set of pictures has the same symbol at the top. Put each set of pictures in order. Then read the nursery rhyme that goes with the pictures.

Humpty Dumpty sat on a wall.

Humpty Dumpty had a great fall.

All the king's horses and all the king's men couldn't put Humpty together again.

The Itsy Bitsy Spider climbed up the waterspout.

Down came the rain and washed the spider out.

Out came the sun and dried up all the rain and the itsy bitsy spider went up the spout again.

Beginning, Middle, and End

Circle the **beginning** of each life cycle with a red crayon.
Circle the **middle** of each life cycle with a green crayon.
Circle the **end** of each life cycle with a blue crayon.

Life Cycle of a Butterfly

Life Cycle of a Frog

Life Cycle of a Chicken

Beginning, Middle, and End

Write a **B** under the picture that shows what happened in the **beginning**.
Write an **M** under the picture that shows what happened in the **middle**.
Write an **E** under the picture that shows what happened in the **end**.

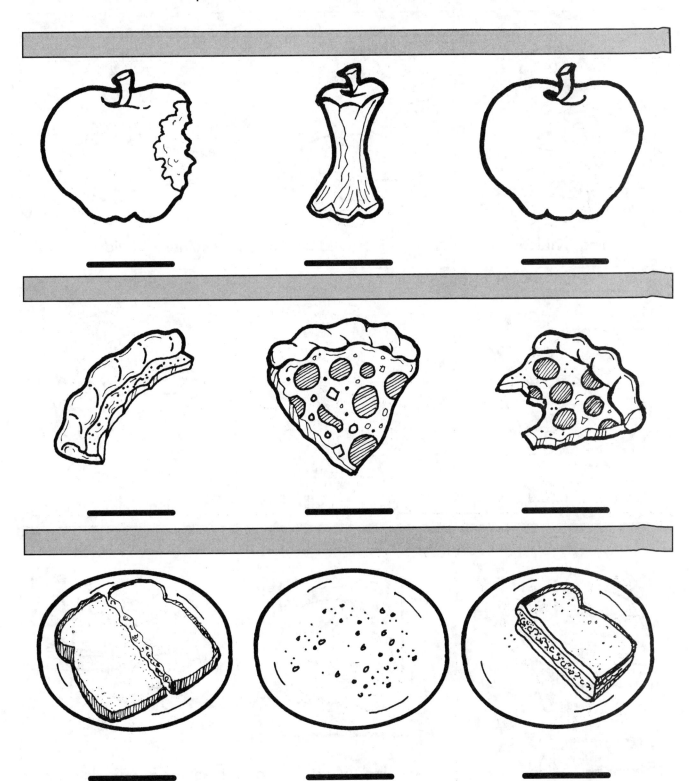

Beginning, Middle, and End

Look **at** the three pictures in each row. Circle the word **Beginning**, **Middle**, or **End** under each picture.

Beginning Middle End   Beginning Middle End   Beginning Middle End

Beginning Middle End   Beginning Middle End   Beginning Middle End

Beginning Middle End   Beginning Middle End   Beginning Middle End

Beginning, Middle, and End (cont.)

Look at the three pictures in each row. Circle the word **Beginning**, **Middle**, or **End** under each picture.

Beginning Middle End   Beginning Middle End   Beginning Middle End

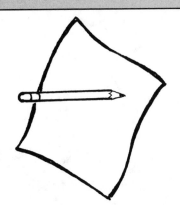  

Beginning Middle End   Beginning Middle End   Beginning Middle End

Beginning Middle End   Beginning Middle End   Beginning Middle End

Ordinal Numbers

Cut out the puzzle pieces on pages 34 and 35. Then put the train cars in order.

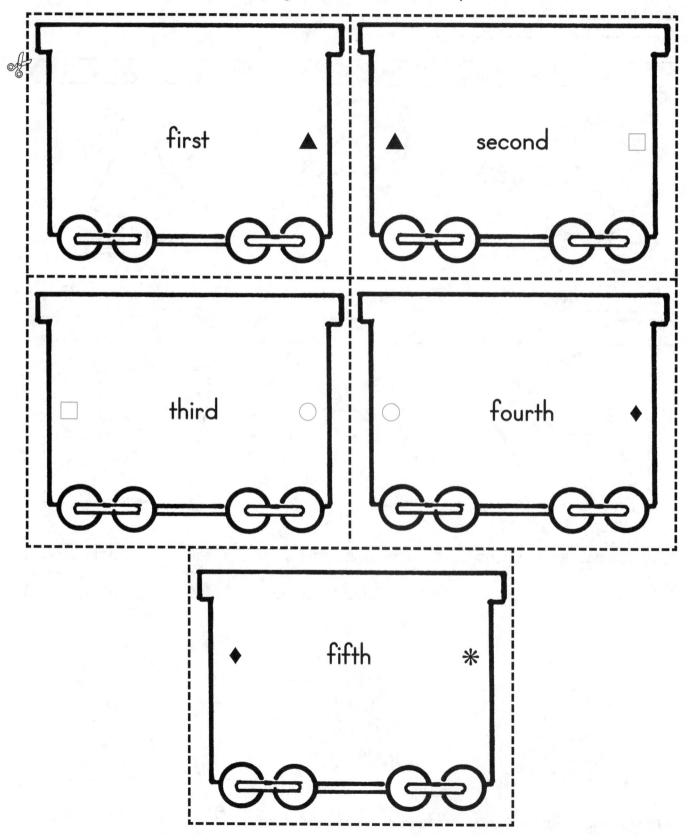

Ordinal Numbers (cont.)

Cut out the puzzle pieces on pages 34 and 35. Then put the train cars in order.

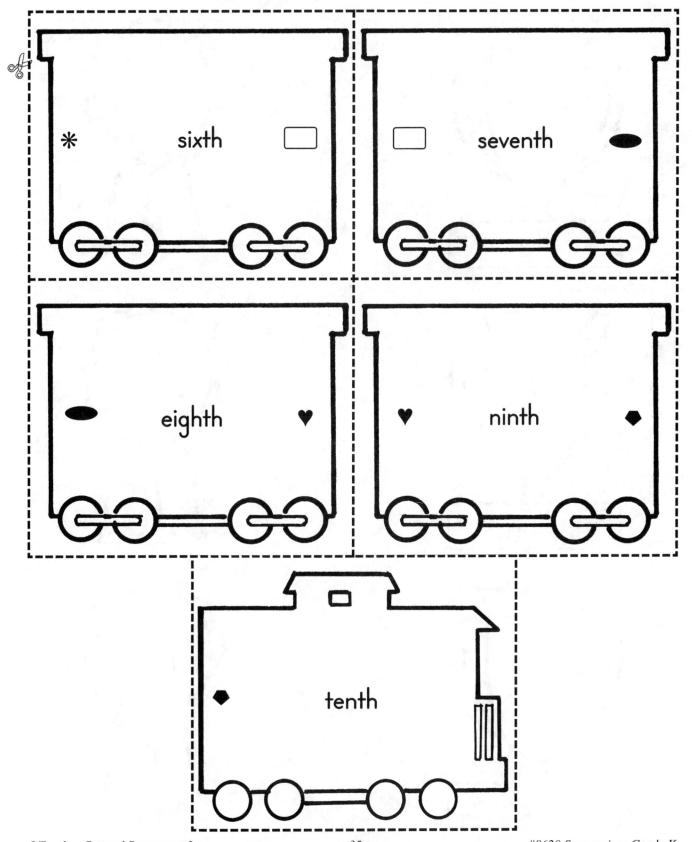

Ordinal Numbers

Draw a line from each trophy to its matching ribbon.

first

second

third

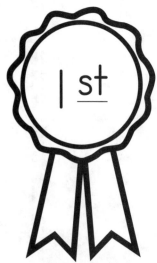

Ordinal Numbers

Look at the clues. Then look at the three children in each row. Use the clues to help you know the order in which the children will line up. Circle the correct ordinal number under each child.

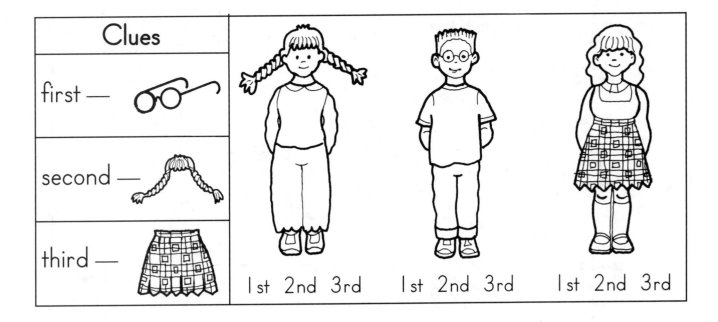

Ordinal Numbers

Look at the pictures in each row.
Draw a circle around the person who is **first**.
Draw a line under the person who is **second**.
Draw an X on the person who is **third**.

Ordinal Numbers

Write an **F** for **first**, an **S** for **second**, and a **T** for **third** under each picture.

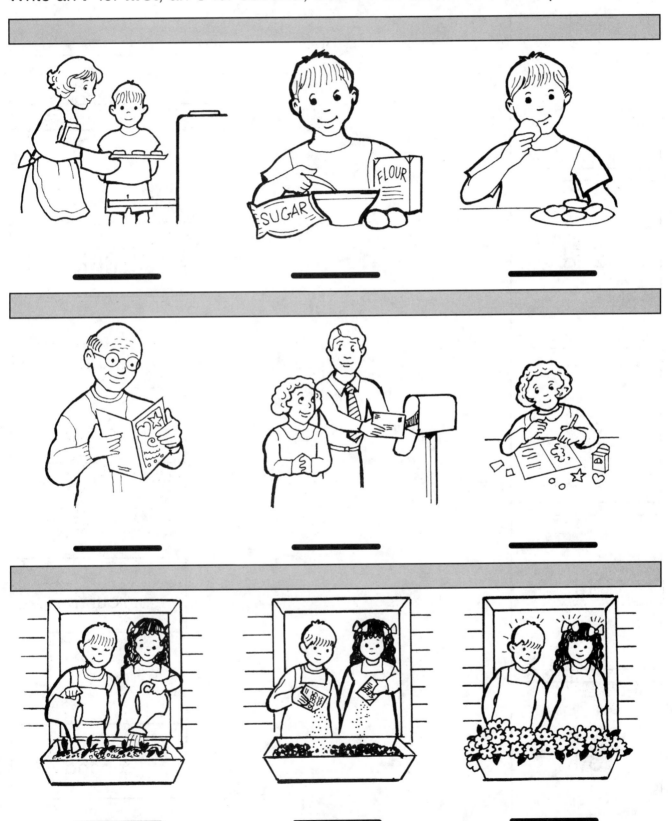

Ordinal Numbers

Draw a line to match each pair of ordinal numbers.

1st	third
2nd	fifth
3rd	first
4th	fourth
5th	second

Ordinal Numbers *(cont.)*

Draw a line to match each pair of ordinal numbers.

6th	ninth
7th	sixth
8th	tenth
9th	eighth
10th	seventh

Ordinal Numbers

Look at the pictures in each row. Circle the word **First**, **Second**, or **Third** under each picture.

First
Second
Third

First
Second
Third

First
Second
Third

First
Second
Third

First
Second
Third

First
Second
Third

Ordinal Numbers

Look at the pictures in each row. Each animal got a ribbon that shows whether it won first, second, or third prize. Write **first**, **second**, or **third** under each picture to match the ribbon.

_____   _____   _____

_____   _____   _____

_____   _____   _____

Answer Key

Page 4

1. C, E

2. F, G, J

3. L, N

4. Q, T, U

5. W, Y, Z

Page 5

1. c,

2. x, z

3. n, o

4. h, i

5. s, t

Pages 6 and 7

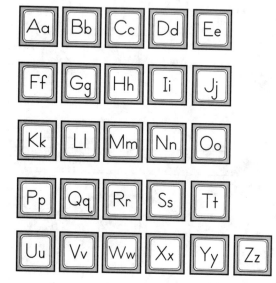

Page 8

A	B	C	D	E
F	G	H	I	J
K	L	M	N	O
P	Q	R	S	T
U	V	W	X	Y
	Z			

Page 9

A a B b C c D d
E e F f G g H h
I i J j K k L l
M m N n O o P p
Q q R r S s T t
U u V v W w X x
Y y Z z

Page 10

1. d, e

2. o, p

3. u, v

4. i, j

5. x, y

Page 11

1. f, g

2. v, w

3. a, b

4. l, m

5. q, r

Answer Key *(cont.)*

Page 12 and 13

Page 14

Page 15

Page 16

Page 17

_4_,5, _6_	G,H, _I_
_6_,7, _8_	A,B, _C_
_1_,2, _3_	W,X, _Y_
_9_,10, _11_	S,T, _U_
_14_,15, _16_	N,O, _P_
_18_,19, _20_	K,L, _M_

Page 18

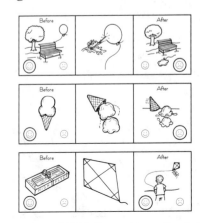

Page 19

Answer Key *(cont.)*

Page 20

Page 21

Page 22

Page 23

Pages 24 and 25

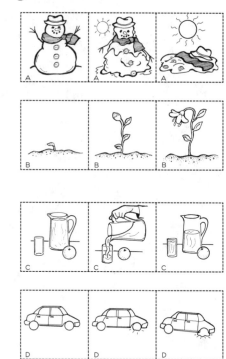

Page 27

Page 28

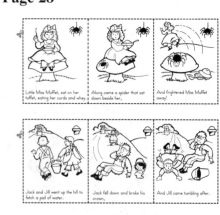

Answer Key *(cont.)*

Page 29

Page 30

Students should draw a circle in the color indicated under each picture.

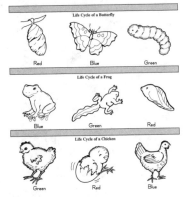

Page 31

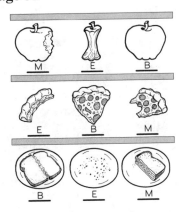

Page 32

Page 33

Pages 34 and 35

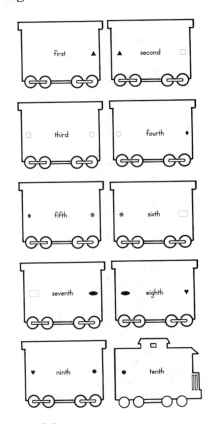

Page 36

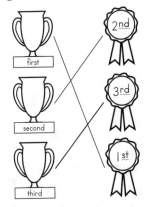

Answer Key *(cont.)*

Page 37

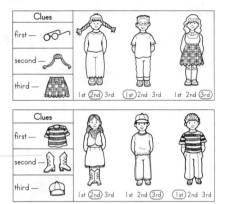

Page 38

Page 39

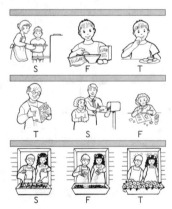

Page 40

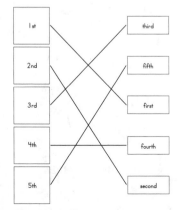

Page 41

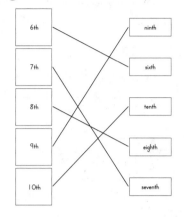

Page 42

Page 43

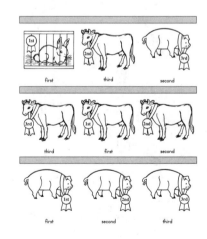